Younger Spotter's Guides
SEASHORE
Su Swallow

Illustrated by John Barber,
Trevor Boyer, Hilary Burn,
Annabel Milne and
Peter Stebbing
Designed by Sally Burrough
and Niki Overy
Edited by Sue Jacquemier and
Jim Roberts

First published in 1978 by Usborne
Publishing Limited, 20 Garrick Street,
London WC2E 9BJ.

Printed in England

USBORNE

D1513919

This book shows some of the animals and plants that you can find on the seashore. Different things live on different kinds of beaches.

Sandy and muddy beaches are good places to look for birds. Many flowers grow on sand dunes. You can find some shells in the sand.

Sandy and muddy beach

On rocky shores look for seaweed and shells on the rocks. Fishes and crabs live in the pools and flowers grow along cliff-tops.

There is less to spot on shingle beaches, but look for seaweed and empty shells washed ashore.

Rocky shore

The best time to explore the seashore is at low tide. If you look under stones or seaweed, put them back carefully. If you pick up an animal, hold it gently and put it back where you found it.

Shells can be empty or they can be alive, with the animals still inside them. Collect only the empty shells.

Shingle beach

When you spot one of the animals or plants in this book, put a tick in the box under its picture.

Sea Holly

This prickly plant grows on sand dunes and stony beaches. Butterflies visit the round blue flowers in summer. Its grey-blue leaves turn white in winter.

Viper's Bugloss

The stems of this plant are covered in sharp hairs. In the summer it has pink buds, but the flowers are blue. Look for this plant on sand dunes.

Seed pods

Bird's Foot Trefoil

Some people call this plant "bacon and eggs" because the flowers are yellow with red streaks. The seed pods are long and black. Look on sand dunes and cliffs.

The flowers look like this

Knotgrass

This plant has tiny pink flowers in the summer and autumn. It spreads over the ground in a thick mat, or grows upright. Look for it on the seashore and in fields.

Common Centaury

You might find this plant on sand dunes, in grassland and even in woods. It grows upright, with pairs of leaves up the stem. Its flowers close at night.

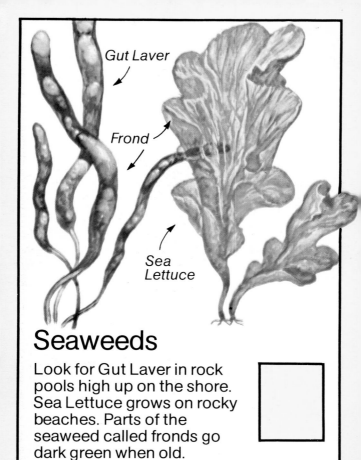

Gut Laver

Frond

Sea Lettuce

Seaweeds

Look for Gut Laver in rock
pools high up on the shore.
Sea Lettuce grows on rocky
beaches. Parts of the
seaweed called fronds go
dark green when old.

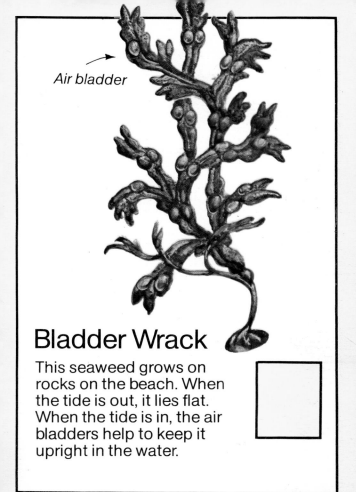

Air bladder

Bladder Wrack

This seaweed grows on
rocks on the beach. When
the tide is out, it lies flat.
When the tide is in, the air
bladders help to keep it
upright in the water.

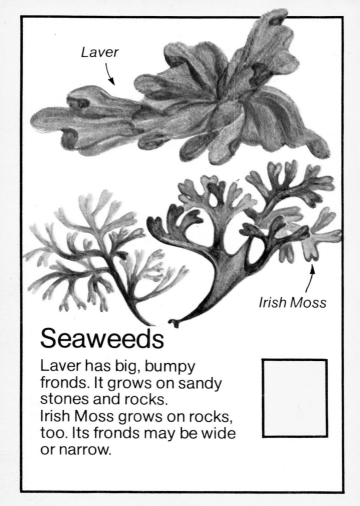

Laver

Irish Moss

Seaweeds

Laver has big, bumpy
fronds. It grows on sandy
stones and rocks.
Irish Moss grows on rocks,
too. Its fronds may be wide
or narrow.

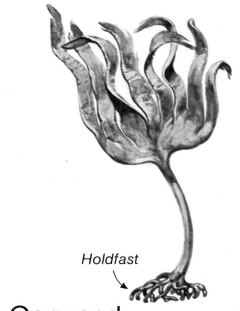

Holdfast

Oarweed

Oarweed is brown and can be one and a half metres long. Look for it in shallow water on rocky beaches.It clings to the rocks with its holdfast.

Herring Gull

This gull is common in fishing ports and seaside towns. It often eats food that people throw away. It nests in groups on cliffs or, sometimes, on buildings.

Black-headed Gull

This gull has a dark brown head in the summer. In winter its head is nearly all white. Its beak and legs are red. It lives near the sea and sometimes inland.

Curlew

The Curlew wades in the water on its long legs. With its long bill, it looks for food in sand and mud. It eats worms and shellfish. It flies inland to nest.

14

Oystercatcher

The Oystercatcher is a wading bird. It wades in the shallow water on sandy beaches. It eats shellfish. It opens the shells with its strong bill.

Redshank

This bird is called Redshank because of its red legs. When it flies, you can see white markings on its back and wings. It lives on muddy shores and wet places.

Young bird

Adult bird

Ringed Plover

This is a small wading bird. It lives on sandy and stony beaches. Notice how it runs about, then stops to feed quickly and runs on again. It nests on the ground.

17

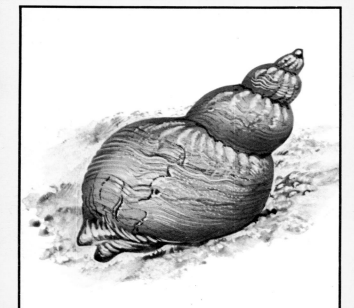

Common Whelk

Look for this large brown shell on sandy and muddy beaches. Sea anemones and sponges sometimes cover it. Hermit Crabs often live in empty Whelk shells.

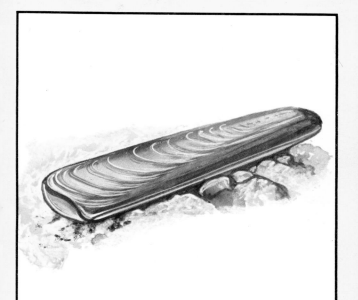

Razor Shell

Some shells bury themselves in the sand. You may find them by digging near the water's edge at low tide. Razor Shells leave hollows where they burrow.

Cockle

Cockles have two shells joined together. Empty shells are often broken apart by the sea. Cockles live in sand and mud.

Limpet

Slipper Limpet

Limpets

Limpets cling to rocks so
tightly that you cannot pull
them off.
Slipper Limpets live on rocks
too. They often live on top of
one another.

Mussel

Periwinkle

Mussel and Periwinkle

Mussels fix themselves to
rocks with thin threads.
People collect them to eat.
Periwinkles live on rocks and
seaweed. Look for them low
down on the beach.

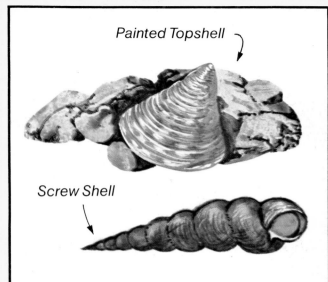

Painted Topshell

Screw Shell

Painted Topshell and Screw Shell

Look for Painted Topshells on rocks. They are yellowy pink with red stripes. Screw Shells do not live on the beach, but empty ones can be washed up there.

Edible Crab

People eat this kind of crab. Small Edible Crabs live in rock pools, under seaweed and buried in the sand. In deep water they grow bigger.

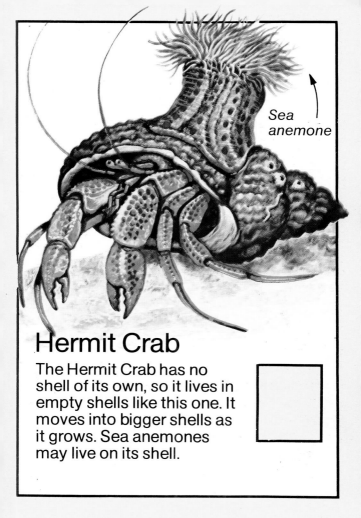

Sea anemone

Hermit Crab

The Hermit Crab has no shell of its own, so it lives in empty shells like this one. It moves into bigger shells as it grows. Sea anemones may live on its shell.

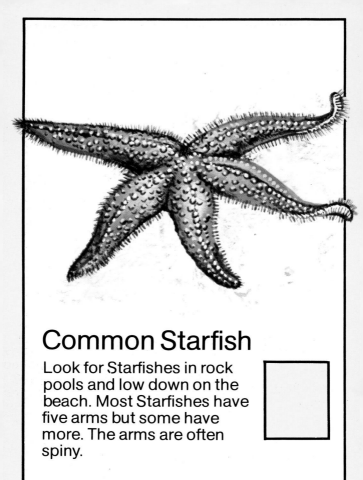

Common Starfish

Look for Starfishes in rock pools and low down on the beach. Most Starfishes have five arms but some have more. The arms are often spiny.

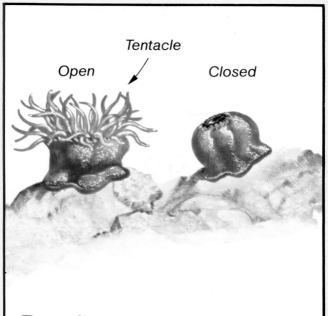

Open *Tentacle* *Closed*

Beadlet Anemone

Sea Anemones are animals, not flowers. Look for them in rock pools. They catch food with their tentacles. When they are out of water their tentacles are drawn in.

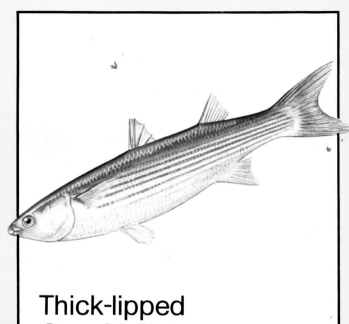

Thick-lipped
Grey Mullet

This fish has a very thick top
lip. Large shoals of Grey
Mullet swim about in
shallow water. They eat
plants and animals that live
on rocks or in the mud.

Ballan Wrasse

Many Wrasses have bright colours. Their colours may change as they get older. This Wrasse lives among rocks. It eats mussels.

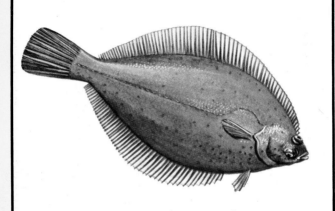

Dab

You might see a Dab when you are paddling on a sandy beach. It hides by flapping its fins to cover itself with sand. It eats small animals with shells.

Worm Pipefish

This long, thin fish hides among seaweed in rock pools. It is not a strong swimmer. The male carries the eggs under its body until they hatch.

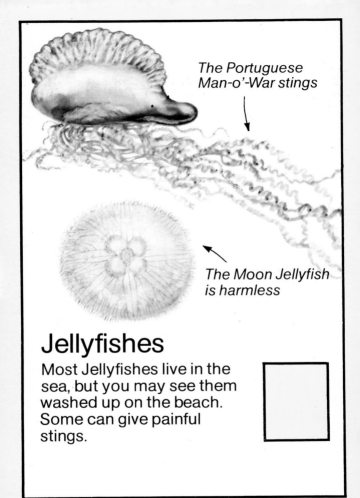

*The Portuguese
Man-o'-War stings*

*The Moon Jellyfish
is harmless*

Jellyfishes

Most Jellyfishes live in the
sea, but you may see them
washed up on the beach.
Some can give painful
stings.